Doll A

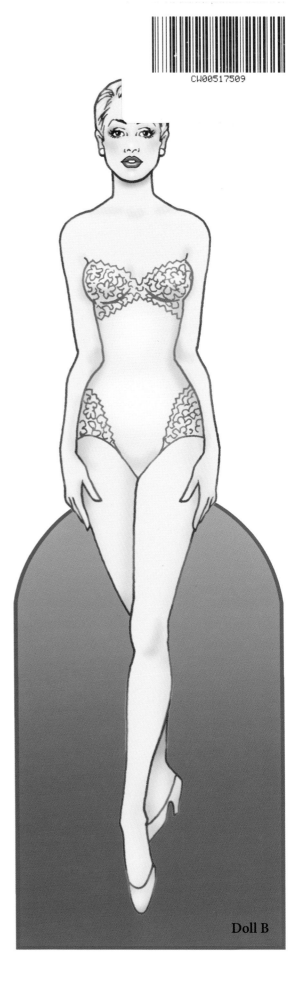

Doll B

PLATE 1

Coco Chanel
1926

Paul Poiret
1910

PLATE 2

Christian Dior
1940s or 1950s

PLATE 3

Do not cut out the white areas between the arms and the body.

Gareth Pugh
2009

Christian Dior
1940s or 1950s

PLATE 4

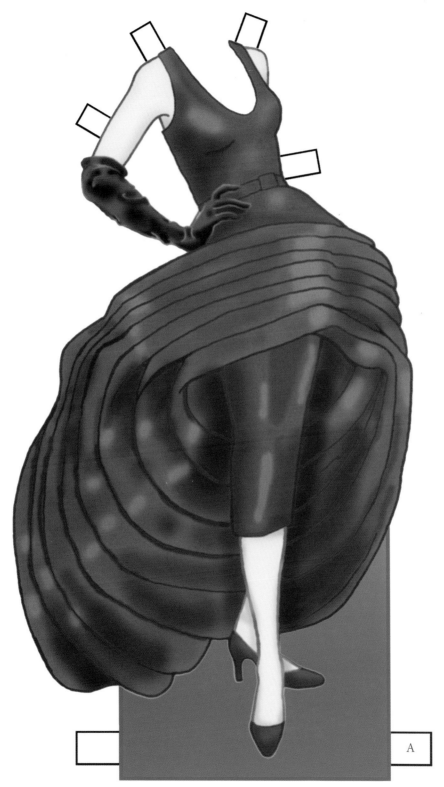

A

Roberto Capucci
"Nine Skirts"
1956

PLATE 5

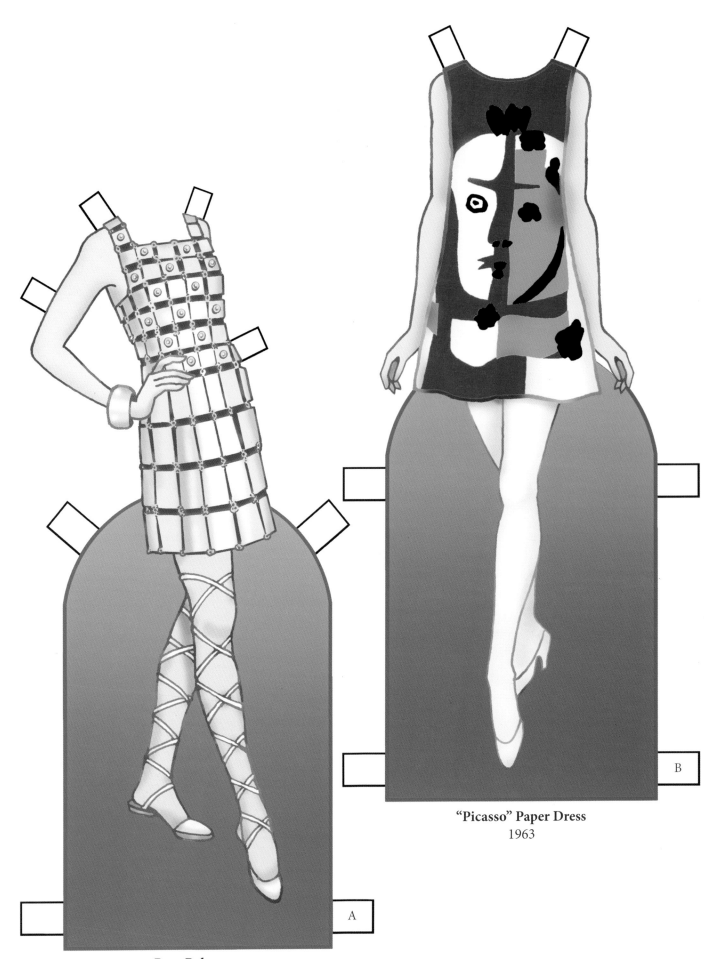

"Picasso" Paper Dress
1963

Paco Rabanne
1960s

B

A

PLATE 6

Yves Saint Laurent
1998

Balenciaga
1965

Plate 7

Do not cut out the
white areas between
the arms and the body.

John Galliano
2000s

PLATE 8

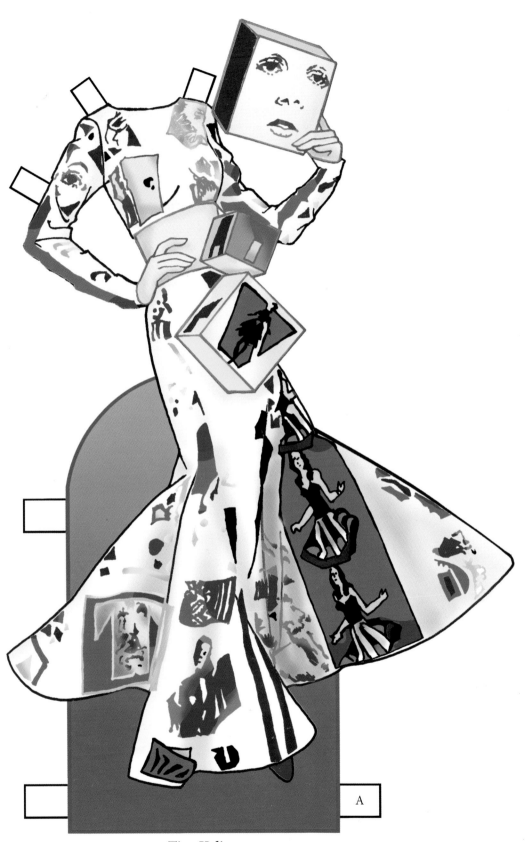

Tina Kalivas
Early 2000s

PLATE 9

Cut out the shape below, and glue
the edge (blue area) to the back
of the headdress. This will form a
pocket for the doll's head.

A

Guo Pei
2008

PLATE 10

B

Do not cut out the
white areas between
the arms and the body.

B

Alexander McQueen
2009

PLATE 11

Do not cut out the white area between the arm and the body.

A

Alexander McQueen
Late 2000s

PLATE 12

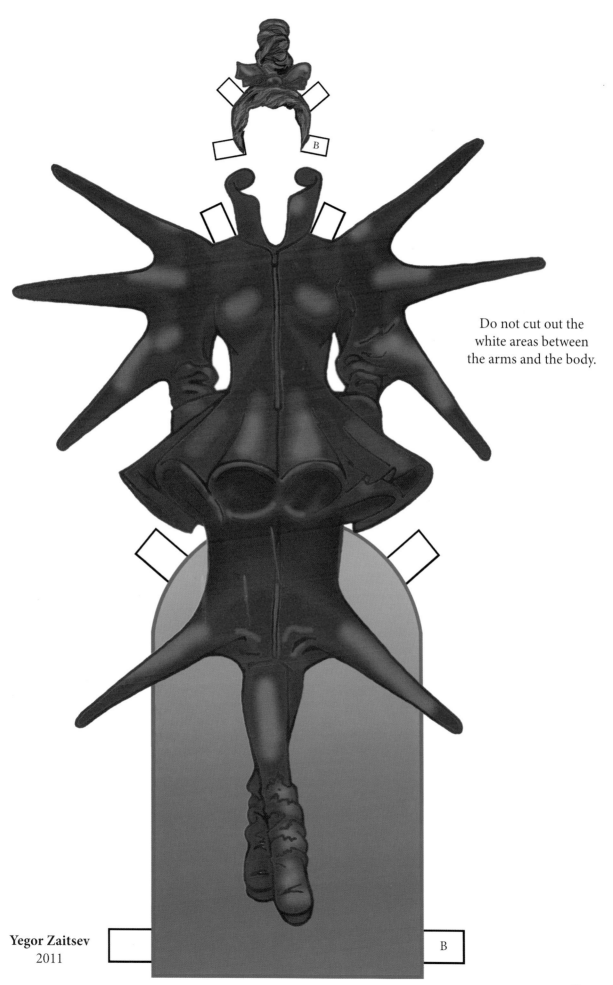

Do not cut out the
white areas between
the arms and the body.

B

B

B

Yegor Zaitsev
2011

PLATE 13

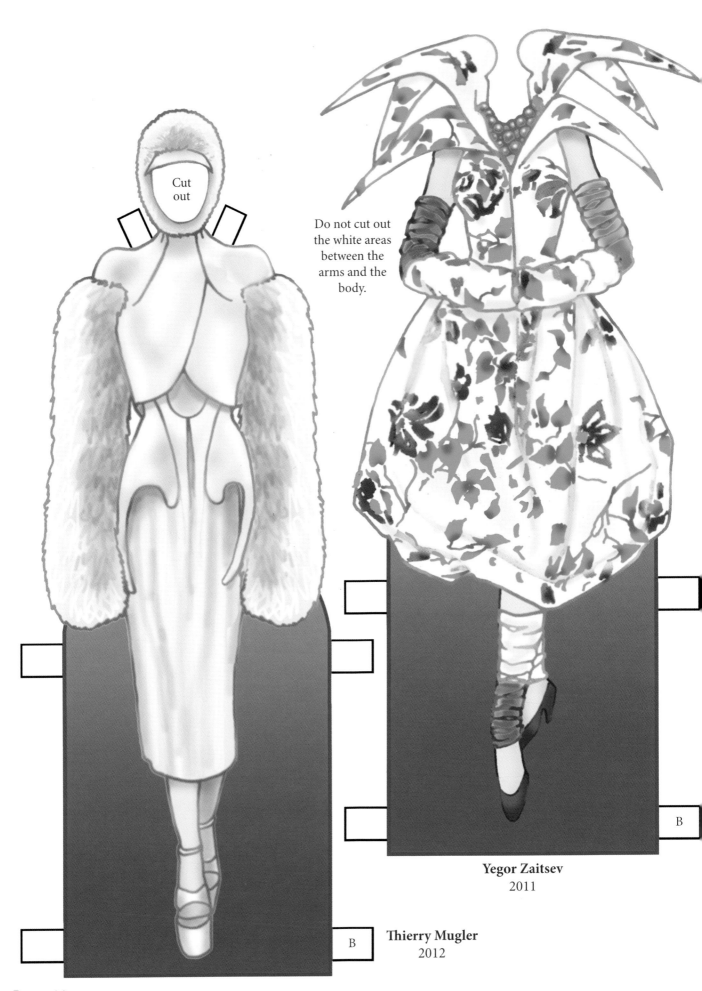

Cut out

Do not cut out the white areas between the arms and the body.

Yegor Zaitsev
2011

Thierry Mugler
2012

B

B

PLATE 14

Do not cut out
the white areas
between the arms
and the body.

B

Gareth Pugh
2009

B

Jean Louis Sabaji
2013

PLATE 15

Cut
out

Do not cut out
the white area
between the arms
and the body.

A

Jan Taminiau
2000s

Tom Ford
2014

PLATE 16